The Art and Science of Viral Social Media Content

Table of Contents

When you've got 5 minutes to fill, Twitter is a great way to fill 35 minutes.

— Matt Cutts

Chapter 1. Introduction

Special Report: The Art and Science of Viral Social Media Content. Ever wondered why certain posts on social media grab your attention while others simply pass by without making so much as a ripple in the digital sea? The answer lies in an exciting blend of creative artistry and strategic science - a combination as riveting as it is effective. In this Special Report, we take a delightful journey exploring this captivating interplay, shedding light on the strategies that allow content creators to pull the perfect heartstrings and push the right online buttons. Discover a world where clever quips meet calculated queues, where engaging emojis dance with data-driven decisions. Are you ready to unravel the secrets of viral social media content and step up your digital game? This comprehensive report holds the fascinating insights you've been seeking, waiting to turn you into the social media whizz you're meant to be!

Chapter 2. Cracking the Virality Code: Understanding What Makes Content 'Click'

The landscape of social media is constituted by an assortment of content but only a proportion of this vast ocean creates genuine waves, becoming 'viral' in nature. We initiate our exploration by embarking on the quest to understand what 'makes the content click', as it were, unraveling the mystic code underlying the virality of social media content.

2.1. The Essence of Virality

Let's begin by encapsulating the meaning of 'virality'. In the simplest terms, a viral piece of content is one that is shared, clicked, or viewed by a colossal number of individuals in a short duration of time. This sharing is not merely a shallow proliferation, but a significant one, characterized by a geometric progression, with every sharer fuelling a cascade of further shares and so forth.

The viral content is akin to a raging wildfire, spreading at an exponential rate through the enormous foliage of the internet, acquiring views, likes, shares, comments, and reactions as it propagates. However, it is crucial to grasp that virality isn't an accident; it is a refined blend of art and science.

2.2. The Virality Conundrum: Art or Science?

As we trudge further into the dissection of this multifaceted virality code, it is helpful to hypothesize virality as a pulsating dance between art and science.

An artist, a fervent creator of content, brings innovation, uniqueness and authenticity into the creation process, thus becoming what we can term as the 'Art' aspect of this paradigm. Simultaneously, a clear comprehension of social media networks, algorithms, timing, trending topics, and psychological triggers manifest the 'Science' aspect.

But was it always this way? Eons ago, in the dawn of the digital age, the 'Art' facet enjoyed unrivaled dominance. Content was significant, period. However, today, 'Art' coexists and collaborates with the 'Science' feature, seeking its assistance to devise strategic content to captivate the correct audience at the right time and in the precise manner.

2.3. The Art & Emotion Quotient in the Virality Code

Art injects emotion into the DNA of the content. A spectrum of emotions: joy, anger, awe, curiosity, surprise, or even consternation can serve as the vehicle for content's stride into virality.

That funny meme, the heart-wrenching story, or the awe-inspiring video - they all engage us, evoke powerful emotions and impel us to share them, contributing to the virality phenomenon.

2.4. The Science & Strategy Quotient in the Virality Code

A diplomatic understanding of the mechanics of social media platforms forms the basis for the 'Science' facet of the virality code. Each social media platform has its unique algorithm that stipulates what content gets seen, when, and by whom. Being viral is not purely serendipitous; timing and targeting are of critical importance. Analyzing the behavior patterns of your audience: when they are most active, what type of content ignites their interest, etc., can lend strategic power to your posts, optimizing them for maximum virality.

Additionally, leveraging trends, hashtags, and understanding the particular linguistic nuances of each platform can amplify the potential of your content to go viral.

2.5. The Symbiosis of Art and Science in the Virality Code

The magical phenomenon of virality marvelously illuminates the synergy between art and science. Inspired artistry can bring to life incredible pieces of content, but without strategic science, their potential remains untapped, akin to words whispered in a whirlwind, lost amidst chaos.

Conversely, to merely mechanically adhere to algorithmic strategies without infusing any authentic creativity is akin to penning a book without a plot, without emotion, without soul. Sure, it may be visible; it might even garner some attention, but it would fail to resonate, to touch hearts, to ripple out in waves of shared sentiment, to go truly viral.

Conclusively, to crack the enigmatic virality code is to discern the poignant dance between art and science, to grasp when to lead with raw, emotive content, and when to trail with strategic science. It's a conversation between authenticity and strategy, a dialogue between emotion and empirical data that together weave the marvelous tapestry of viral content.

By apprehending this delicate balance, you will not only understand what makes content 'click,' but also gain the power to inspire it to do so - the key to unlock indomitable viral waves, to compel content to sizzle and skyrocket in the infinite galaxy of social media.

Chapter 3. The Science of Attention: Psychological Triggers for Engagement

3.1. Understanding the Human Mind: The Powerhouse Behind Attention

Social media, an arena ever bustling with bytes of information, is in a fierce competition for the most precious resource - the attention of users. To understand how to capture this hot commodity, we must first dive into the intricacies of the human mind.

Ourselves, as biological organisms, are built for survival. Evolutionarily speaking, our brains tend to focus more intently on stimuli that might be critical to our wellbeing. In the online context, this equates to content that arouses emotional responses or reflects our interests and motivations. Knowing this, the strategic content creator crafts posts that can pierce through the armour of indifference and make one's grey cells sit up and take notice.

3.2. Emotional Triggers: The Heart of the Matter

But what really is an 'emotional trigger'? It is any topic, event, or sentiment that sparks a significant emotional response. Different emotions can serve unique purposes in the digital landscape, and understanding the whole spectrum is crucial for the virality of content.

Joy, surprise, anger, sadness - these are the four basic emotions that have been cited as the pillars of virality. Posts that evoke these feelings tend to have a higher chance of being shared because they resonate at a fundamental human level.

Furthermore, researchers at the University of Pennsylvania found that positive content generally outperforms the negative. Content that incites positive emotions, like joy or awe, inspires users to share, spreading positivity in their social circle.

However, negative emotional triggers also have their place in the canon. Content invoking anger or anxiety can prompt shares fueled by a sense of injustice or urgency. News content or social issues often capitalize on this aspect.

3.3. Social Proof and Reciprocity: The Invisible Hands Shaping Engagement

Online, we're part of a vast, interconnected web of individuals. Two powerful psychological phenomena at play within this realm are the principles of 'Social Proof' and 'Reciprocity'.

'Social Proof' is a phenomenon where people base their actions on what others are doing. It's the herd mentality in action. If a post is popular, the chances are it will continue to gain popularity because its high engagement levels suggest it's valuable. This is why influencers or celebrities can garner large amounts of attention; they operate as the guiding light towards which their audience gravitates.

On the other side, 'Reciprocity' relies on the tit-for-tat principle. If user A likes or shares user B's content, user B will feel a subconscious obligation to do the same. Facebook's "People you may know" feature and Instagram's "Suggested for you" function, where users are prompted to follow others who follow them, both exploit this principle splendidly.

3.4. FOMO: The Fear that Fuels Engagement

Next in line is the concept of FOMO - Fear Of Missing Out. This powerful psychological trigger works by instilling a sense of urgency and scarcity, compelling users to engage immediately lest they miss out on an experience or a piece of information that others are enjoying.

Trending hashtags, limited-time-only deals, breaking news, 'live' status updates - they all exploit this fear. The effect is often amplified when influencers or widely-followed figures are involved. For businesses, utilizing this tactic can result in waves of impulse engagements and shares.

3.5. Exclusivity and The Cocktail Party Effect: Making the User Feel Special

Lastly, we discuss the power of 'Exclusivity' and 'The Cocktail Party Effect'. This arguably elite duo works on the notion that people crave unique experiences and personalized communication.

Exclusivity can be offered in the form of limited-edition offerings, insider access, or privileged memberships. It sparks intrigue, an irresistible magnet for attention.

The 'Cocktail Party Effect', a term rooted in auditory attention research, describes the phenomenon where, amid a chaotic cocktail party, you can tune out all other voices the moment your name is called out. On social media, this may translate into personalized posts or direct user engagements, which have a higher chance of gaining attention, as the user feels seen, recognized, and valued.

In conclusion, these psychological triggers affect how people perceive and interact with social media content. Mastery of these triggers coupled with a keen sense of audience understanding can significantly enhance one's capacity to produce truly engaging, viral content.

Chapter 4. Harnessing The Art of Storytelling: Narratives That Echo Online

Storytelling has long been the thread that weaves tales, binds societies, and undoubtedly, it remains a vital component of human communication. It could be argued that social media has amplified storytelling's importance even more, as the capability to make content resonate with audiences online depends on an effective narrative. This capacity to capture an audience's attention, to make them care about the subject matter at hand and to inspire action, is what storytelling in the digital age inherently aspires.

4.1. Understanding the Power of Storytelling

From our early ancestors gathering around the fire, sharing tales of their days to modern Netflix binges, storytelling remains a constant. It's more than a source of entertainment; it's a potent form of communication. And surely, understanding its power is key to leveraging storytelling for enhancing online engagement.

Akin to a story told around a campfire, viral content needs to engage its audience on an emotional level. This emotional engagement stands as the fundamental driving force for social sharing. Humans are biologically wired to respond to stories - we empathize, connect, and relate to narratives, and social media exposes us to a plethora of them every day. Hence, mastering the art of storytelling is indispensable in the digital age.

4.2. The Elements of an Engaging Story

Crafting an engaging narrative involves technical artistry and a generous dose of creative flair. But let's not get lost in the abstract, let's inspect the concrete elements that foster an engaging story online:

1. A Clear, Compelling Beginning: Every story needs a hook, something to snag the audience's interest and pique curiosity. A powerful opening statement, a provocative question, or an unexpected twist can serve as this hook, inviting viewers to succumb to the allure of your narrative.

2. Authentic Characters and Plots: Authenticity breeds connection. Genuine characters and believable plots facilitate audience immersion, making them care about your narrative's trajectory.

3. Conflict and Resolution: These two elements establish the story's heart. Conflict draws viewers in, making them invested, while resolution gives them satisfaction, rounding off the narrative beautifully.

4. Consistent Tone and Style: A coherent voice enables your brand to form its distinctive identity, allowing your audiences to cultivate a familiar relationship with your content.

4.3. Crafting Stories for Social Media

The endless stream of content on social media demands special consideration for storytelling. A story that resonates on Facebook might not ring as loudly on Twitter due to distinct audience preferences and platform-specific features. Consequently, understanding the nuances of each platform and tailoring your narratives accordingly stands as key for successful online engagement.

Here are some steps to craft resonant social media stories:

1. Identify Your Audience: Understand who your followers are and craft your story in a way that speaks directly to them. This involves understanding their interests, concerns, and values and reflect these in your narrative.

2. Incorporate Visual Elements: A picture paints a thousand words - a truth that remains starkly manifest in social media. Utilize graphics, videos, and other visual tools to enrich your storytelling.

3. Employ Sequential Storytelling: Sequential stories or multi-part stories help create anticipation and encourage audience engagement over time.

4. Encourage Interaction: Including polls, questions, or calls to action can encourage interaction, further solidifying the connection between your brand and your audience.

4.4. Strategies for Amplifying Your Story's Reach

Producing a stellar story doesn't ensure virality. To amplify its reach, consider these strategies:

1. Leverage Influencers: Collaborating with influencers in your field can help you reach a larger audience with your narrative. The endorsement of your story by an influencer can instill a sense of trust and increase its reach.

2. Use Reliable Data: Data-driven storytelling increases credibility and can make complicated topics more relatable. Embed relevant data and statistics within your narrative to reinforce your message.

3. Encourage Shares: Prompt your audience to share your content. User engagement fosters a sense of community and can attract

more viewers.

4. Optimize for SEO: Including appropriate keywords and hashtags can help your story surface in relevant searches, spreading it to a wider audience.

Harnessing the art of storytelling in social media isn't merely a strategy, but an ongoing journey. It involves understanding, experimentation, and an ever-evolving process of engaging your audience with creatively crafted tales. With authentic narratives that echo online, you hold the power to turn whispers into roars, shaping the endless sea of digital content with your resonant ripples.

Chapter 5. Mastering Memes and Emojis: The New Language of the Internet

In our newfound era of digitization, traditional linguistic cues have been transformed and expanded, leading to the birth of a new language - the language of memes and emojis. This unique and ever-evolving form of communication has reshaped how interactions happen on the internet, providing users with innovative tools to express emotions and ideas. Crafting and deploying memes and emojis with finesse is an essential expertise for the modern digital communicator. In the following sections, we delve into the intricate details of this craft.

5.1. The Intriguing World of Memes

Memes, an inherent digital cultural phenomenon, are pieces of content, almost like a digital genetic code, that are spread, adapted, and evolved by internet users. They're humorous, they're relatable, and more importantly, they're shareable.

Derived from the Greek word 'mimema', which means 'what is imitated', memes are broadly defined as concepts, behaviours or ideas that spread from person to person within a culture. Coined by Richard Dawkins in his book 'The Selfish Gene', the term 'meme' has transformed over decades to denote an activity, concept, or piece of media that spreads, often as mimicry or humorous instances, from person to person via the Internet.

As internet inhabitants, we are all well versed in the emotionally cathartic, social bonding and opinion-forming power of memes. They offer a framework for shared understanding, providing a shorthand to complicated feelings or deeply entrenched cultural norms that thousands can relate to. And in this sheer relatability and shareability lies their potential for virality.

5.2. The Emotive Power of Emojis

From a teary-eyed laughter face to a dancing red lady, emojis, the colourful pictographs we regularly pepper our messages, emails, and social media posts with, aren't just fun; they represent an evolution in language.

Originally hailing from Japan, the term 'emoji' translates to 'picture word'. These digital pictographs have evolved from simple emoticons (like the classic text-based smiley, :-)) to a panoply of faces, symbols, and objects that we use to add flavor to our digital communications.

Emojis enrich our messages, providing emotional subtext, tone, and nuance, thus overcoming some of the limitations posed by text-based communication. In essence, emojis add a personal touch to our digital messages, making them more human.

5.3. Crafting Virality With Memes and Emojis

Combining the communal nature of memes and the emotional resonance of emojis can prove potent in crafting content that clicks with audiences and prompts sharing. This paves the path to virality.

Creating memes that resonate requires a keen understanding and agile application of current trends, pop culture references, and niche humor which tap into the collective psyche of your target demographic. Using emojis, on the other hand, involves choosing those that best express the emotional undertone of your message, not just to add color, but to enhance understanding and create connection.

5.4. Manifesting Memes and Emojis in Your Social Media Strategy

To master this new language of the internet and incorporate it into your social media strategy, you must understand your audience, and the shared cultural context within which they operate. You should also comprehend that these digital tools come with the duality of being informal yet impactful.

Understanding the cultural nuances that govern the use of memes and emojis can be a game-changer in achieving online success. The goal is to use these tools in such a way that you not only retain your brand's identity and core message but also foster an interactive space where your audience feels seen, understood, and valued.

5.5. Creating a Meme: Mechanics and Strategy

Creating a meme involves a blend of creativity, strategy, and subtle manipulation. The idea is to understand the current trend, utilize humor, create a relatable content piece that resonates with your audience, and prompt sharing. From inception to execution, meme-making involves multiple steps:

1. Identifying Trending Topics

2. Crafting a Catchy Caption

3. Framing a Relatable Situation

4. Designing Engaging Visuals

5. Sharing & Encouraging Sharing

5.6. Making Effective Use of Emojis

Choosing the right emoji is crucial to communicate effectively in the digital language. In this process, it is important to consider aspects such as cultural differences, potential ambiguities, and audience interpretation. Aim to clarify and enhance your message, rather than confuse your audience with incorrect or excessive use.

In conclusion, mastering the art and science of memes and emojis necessitates creativity, cultural competency, and a keen sensitivity towards the nuances of digital communication. Striking the right balance isn't always easy, but with practice and strategic thinking, you'll be well on your way to viral content creation.

Chapter 6. Hashtag Alchemy: Turning Social Media Messages into Gold

In the world of social media, hashtags serve as powerful tools capable of transforming average, everyday content into viral sensations that captivate audiences worldwide. These nifty, ubiquitous set of characters, led by the now-iconic '#', act as anchors allowing messages to float above the constant flux of the digital information ocean and catch the attention of even the most casual explorer.

6.1. The Birth and Evolution of Hashtags

The humble hashtag grew from a simple categorizing tool introduced by Twitter in 2007. Seeing this function as a way for users to group topics of interest, Twitter software engineer Chris Messina used the pound (#) symbol followed by a word or phrase, a habit borrowed from IRC channels. This marked the birth of the first hashtag - #barcamp.

From its simple inception, the humble hashtag has grown into a full-fledged communication powerhouse. It's been adopted across virtually all major social media platforms, including Facebook, Instagram, LinkedIn, Pinterest, and more. Its usage has evolved to suit the unique characteristics and user demands of each platform, resulting in a rich and varied landscape of hashtagging strategies that can, and should, be leveraged by any serious digital dweller.

6.2. The Science Behind Hashtags: When and Why They Work

Hashtags work by connecting and amplifying messages in the crowded environment of social media. They help surface your content to broader audiences, breaking barriers and transcending your own follower count. Indeed, it's important to understand the science behind them. They act as clickable links, grouping all posts sharing these hashtags.

Yet, their true power lies beyond this simple utility. On psychological terms, hashtags are akin to triggers, catching the eye and inciting curiosity. Moreover, for many users, well-placed hashtags provide a level of social acknowledgment and validation. Those who use a trending hashtag wisely or creatively get to share in that topic's popularity, and their content's visibility rises accordingly.

Indeed, the choice of your hashtags carries significant weight. One needs to walk a fine line between choosing popular hashtags that already have a large following, thus guaranteeing a certain level of visibility, and more niche hashtags that offer less competition.

6.3. Strategies for Effectively Using Hashtags

Successful hashtag use requires more than just attaching a '#' before your message. It requires research, creativity, timing, and sometimes, a touch of luck. Here are aspects to consider:

- Understand your audience: As with any other aspect of content creation, understanding your audience is pivotal. Observe the hashtags your audience is using and interacting with, and try to incorporate these into your posts.

- Research trending hashtags: Being aware of trending hashtags, both globally and within your niche, is of immense help. But be careful. Ensure these hashtags align occasionally with your brand's messaging and target audience.

- Create branded hashtags: A branded hashtag is a fantastic way of creating a digital hub for your content, making it easily searchable for followers. Additionally, a catchy and relevant branded hashtag can become a trending topic, thus raising your brand's visibility.

- Less is more: While it may be tempting to hashtag the whole dictionary, research shows that posts with a reasonable number of hashtags (around 11 on Instagram, for example) tend to perform better.

6.4. Case Studies: Hashtag Alchemy in Practice

While theory and strategy are well and wonderful, it's always helpful to learn from the masters. From #BlackLivesMatter sparking global conversations around racial justice to #ShareACoke transforming a marketing campaign into a viral sensation, and the self-deprecating #fail see-sawing between humor and advice, these case studies give us a glimpse into the transformative power of the ordinary hashtag when brilliantly wielded.

In conclusion, the hashtag is far more than a mere social media tool. It's tiny, yet potent; a bridge that connects you with the right audience; a beacon that guides this audience to your content. Hashtag use is an art as much as it is a science, and mastering it could very well turn your social media messages into shining nuggets of digital gold.

Chapter 7. Whispers into Shouts: Multiplying Reach Through Sharing and Networking

In an age where everyone and anyone can become a content creator, it's crucial to understand effective ways of reaching out to potential viewers and keeping them engaged. This understanding will culminate in realizing the power of whispers transforming into shouts, a metaphor that encapsulates the journey of an idea from conception to being the talk of the town.

7.1. The Theory of Networking and Sharing

Networking and sharing are two primary components in the practice of making a post go viral on social media. Networking refers to creating and nurturing connections with individuals, groups, or institutions who can help disseminate the content. Sharing, on the other hand, involves the strategic proliferation of the content to your existing network and beyond.

In simpler terms, if one can imagine the glorious world of social media as an ever-expanding universe, then each individual, business account, group page, or platform functions as a star within it. All these entities are interlinked, creating a vast network that triggers a domino effect of sharing content, sparking the exciting transformation of whispers into shouts.

7.2. The Art of Social Connections

The art of creating connections requires both strategy and organic interaction. It starts with identifying the relevant individuals or groups who would find your content valuable. These could be people with shared interests or similar beliefs, professionals from the same field, influencers in your area of work or interest, or even organizations that resonate with your content. Remember, networking is not just about quantity but is rather rooted in quality, in fostering relationships that are likely to generate engagement.

On social media platforms, engagement can be calculated based on likes, shares, comments, or reposts. However, in the grand scheme of things, these actions hold a higher value than what meets the eye. Every interaction is a signal, a promotion of sorts, pushing your content into the limelight. Think of these as positive interactions that amplify your content's reach, thereby boosting chances of virality.

7.3. Sharing Mechanisms and Their Algorithms

Sharing strategies greatly hinge on the algorithms of different social platforms. Each platform - Facebook, Twitter, Instagram, LinkedIn, YouTube, Pinterest - has its own algorithm that determines how posts are shared and displayed. Some prioritize personal connections, others leverage user interest, and still, others highlight the popularity or freshness of content.

To harness the power of these algorithms, one needs to understand and adapt to them, mapping out a sharing strategy that aligns with the platform's workings. Staying updated on major algorithm changes can significantly impact the reach and engagement of a post.

7.4. Unlocking the Power of Collaboration and Cross-Promotion

Another pathway to practically manifest the concept of whispers turning into shouts is through collaboration and cross-promotion. Collaboration brings together different content creators, leveraging their individual follower bases, while cross-promotion involves mutual agreement between creators or businesses to promote each other's work.

These strategies don't just multiply the reach of content, they particularly help in reaching new and diverse audiences. Keep in mind, the key to successful collaboration or cross-promotion is essential to have a clear, mutual agreement, and to ensure both parties share similar values and audience demographics to keep the content relevant and effective.

7.5. The Impact of User Engagement

Lastly, in accelerating the whisper-to-shout transformation, one's audience plays a pivotal role. Their engagement turns the wheels of virality, pushing content from one network to another within the vast digital continuum, evolving from simple personal sharing to wider community engagement.

Not only does this engagement boost visibility and reach, but it also adds a layer of authenticity and trust as endorsements come from peers rather than the content creators themselves. User engagement has the potential to be the kingpin in the viral content game, which is why encouraging comments, shares, likes, and other types of interactions should be an integral part of any content strategy.

This journey of whispers turning into shouts is testament to the truly captivating power of social platforms. By carefully mastering the craft of networking and sharing, one can indeed amass a wider

audience, thereby inching ever closer to achieving the golden touch
of virality.

Chapter 8. Adding the Personal Touch: Utilizing User-Generated Content for Authenticity

In the abundantly interconnected digital ecosphere we inhabit these days, the lines between content creators and content consumers have grown significantly blurred. Today, as we adeptly navigate the multiverse of social media, we face a crucial turning point, where we must leverage the power of user-generated content (UGC) for authenticity.

8.1. Entering the Realm of User-Generated Content

UGCs are any form of content such as images, videos, text, and audio that have been posted by users on online platforms. It's an authentic testament to user experiences, feelings, and opinions about a brand or product. The magic of UGC rests in its inherently human element. It beautifully breaks the barrier of corporate speech and resaleable advertising, offering resonance through shared experiences among users.

As an audience, we are more likely to trust the opinions of our peers than the claims of a commercial. Utilizing UGC in content creation facilitates an organic way to build and amplify this trust. It enriches our storytelling, adds richness to our narrative, and deepens our connection with the viewer in a personal dialogue, consequently fostering authenticity.

8.2. The Power of Authenticity in User-Generated Content

Content authenticity has always been critical, but in today's discerning digital landscape, its importance has never been more profound. Consumers are craving real, relatable, and raw content, which has a genuine ability to rise above the deafening noise of clickbait and spam. Brands that can provide this authenticity through UGC are finding themselves at the forefront of their audience's digital consciousness.

This type of content doesn't just exhibit honesty, but it also overlays an organic texture to brand stories that scripted, meticulously polished brand content often lacks. The authenticity that evolves from genuine user experiences becomes the brand's most credible testimonial, boosting its image, credibility, and in turn, user trust.

8.3. Capitalizing on UGC: An Exercise in Responsiveness

A key aspect of implementing UGC in your content strategy is a well-rounded understanding and acceptance of your audience's voice. The conversation is no longer one-way. This paradigm shift requires brands to be attentive, responsive, and adaptive with their audience.

It is crucial to be ever-vigilant for emerging content trends among your followers. They're not just your audience; they are content creators, critics, and ambassadors all at once. By staying attuned to the pulse of your audience's generated content, you can tap into relevant trends, generate new ideas that speak directly to your viewers' tastes, and curate content that truly resonates.

8.4. Implementing UGC: A Trifecta of Consultation, Collaboration, and Creation

UGC can be woven into your content strategy in various forms. Be it through a curated interactive photo or video contest, sharing customer testimonials or reviews, or encouraging user-devised hashtags. The possibilities are as vast and varied as your user base itself.

However, the most critical aspect of utilizing UGC lies in the trifecta of consultation, collaboration, and creation. The user's voice, when integrated seamlessly with the brand's message, can create a uniquely personalized narrative that strikes a chord with the viewer. Journeying together on this path of content creation, brands can foster a sense of community that empowers the audience while simultaneously amplifying their brand impact.

8.5. Challenges in Using UGC

While envelope-pushing and paradigm-shifting, incorporating UGC into mainstream content strategy isn't without its challenges. These include issues related to content moderation, maintaining a consistent brand image while leveraging diverse user content, and copyright concerns.

Having a clear strategy to address these challenges is crucial. This might involve establishing guidelines for UGC, having dedicated teams or technology to curate and verify user content, and being transparent about any modifications made to the original content.

8.6. The Future of UGC

The world of UGC is ever-burgeoning and holds immense potential in the realm of social media content. As users become more influential, their voices loud and clear, we find ourselves perched at the cusp of new ways of thinking and creating.

Brand stories aren't just about the brand anymore. They are about the user, the customer, the viewer, who now share the stage in shaping these narratives. As authenticity becomes the new currency in the digital world, UGC emerges as a goldmine waiting to be explored.

In conclusion, utilizing user-generated content helps humanize your brand, fosters a sense of community, and nurtures trust in the digital landscape. Although UGC presents its challenges, with the right approach, it provides unprecedented opportunities for brands to connect on a profoundly personal level in today's hyper-connected world. Cultivating authenticity has never been more vital or more attainable than it is right now. So, leverage the power of UGC - only then can you truly engage, inspire, and endure in this ever-evolving social media sphere.

Chapter 9. Data-Driven Decision-Making in Content Creation: Use of Analytics and Metrics

Right off the bat, one must understand that the generation of content, far from being an arbitrary process, is more strategically aligned than ever in the age of big data. Data-driven decision-making represents a seismic shift in the approach towards content creation – one that sets a new benchmark for accuracy, efficiency, and adaption in a constantly evolving digital world. It represents the merging of the creative fields with the unequivocal precision of data science.

9.1. The Power of Analytics and Metrics

The vast swath of the internet unfurling before the eyes entails an immense pool of data ripe for analysis. This is where Analytics come in, converting these complex data forms into comprehensible, actionable insights. Metrics, on the other hand, are quantifiable measures used to track and assess the status of a specific process. They serve as the vehicles that drive us from mere data collection towards yielding actionable knowledge.

In the context of social media content, analytics could range from understanding user demographics to user behaviour and beyond. Metrics could differ based on the specific goal of the content, such as tracking shares, likes, comments, reach, impressions, click-through rates, and others. Understanding, applying, and interpreting these analytics and metrics are fundamental to data-driven decision making.

However, the utilization of these analytics and metrics is non-trivial. They must be used within a well-defined strategy to generate value and deliver insights that can guide your content creation process.

9.2. Implementing Strategic Data Analysis

The key to successful data-driven decision-making lies firstly in the identification of the right metrics and secondly in the correct interpretation of data. This begins with the setting of clear objectives that define what you want to achieve, be it increased engagement, wider reach, or conversion of followers into customers. Your objectives will dictate which metrics are the most useful to track and analyze.

Once the metrics to track have been identified, the complex process of data analysis unfolds. This can be broadly distilled into three steps: data collection, data processing, and data interpretation.

1. Data Collection: This involves gathering the relevant data. With various social media platforms offering built-in analytics tools, tracking the data you need is made easier. For instance, Facebook Insights and Twitter Analytics provide invaluable insights into your content performance.

2. Data Processing: Processing raw data is akin to distilling chaos into order. It's filtering the chaff from the wheat - separating the signal from the noise. It involves cleaning, integrating, and transforming raw data to make it suitable for analysis.

3. Data Interpretation: The final, crucial step. It's where you draw meaningful conclusions from the processed data. It's deciphering what your data is trying to tell you about your content performance. This is where true insights that can guide future action are gleaned.

It's an iterative and dynamic process that needs constant tweaking and fine-tuning. Analysis isn't meant to be stagnant; instead, it must ebb and flow with the changing waves of your engagement, adapting as your audience does.

9.3. Utilizing Analytics and Metrics for Content Creation

Data analysis alone is not enough. To create content that resonates with your audience and achieves your objectives, you must apply these analytical findings. Pay close attention to the patterns and trends. They don't lie about what works and what doesn't.

Identify what led to a spike in engagement. Was it the type of content? The time it was posted? The language used? These patterns can give you a blueprint for success, serving as a guide for future content creation.

Simultaneously, metrics can reveal the areas that need improvement. Discern what led to poor engagement. Can you trace it back to the type of content? Or was it the timing? Studying these troughs in performance can help you unravel what to avoid.

In the realm of social media where change is perhaps the only constant, analytics and metrics can give you the agility to navigate these shifts. It's about listening to the data and adapting swiftly.

The beauty of data-driven decision making is that it's a never-ending learning process. It allows you to evolve and refine your strategies consistently. It's harnessing the vast sea of data into a navigational tool, guiding your creative vessel towards the shore of engagement and success.

9.4. Why Going Data-Driven Matters

The beauty of the digital era is that almost everything is measurable. With digital analytics and metrics, while we might be swimming in a pool of data, we also have the ability to decode this information into valuable, practical insights.

Including data-driven decision making in your content strategy is no longer an option; it's a necessity. Ignoring data is comparable to sailing blind, without a compass or map to guide your way. It's neglecting the years of documented user behaviour and trend insights just waiting to be tapped.

Ultimately, data-driven decision-making enhances the odds of your content success, refines your strategy, and saves both time and money. It can propel you forward in the digital race, keeping you responsive and resilient amidst the ebb and flow of the social media currents. It leaves no room for second-guessing as you are guided by clear facts extracted from data about what works best for your audience.

In the puzzle of creating viral content, analytics, and metrics are the missing pieces that complete the picture. They evidence the triumphs and expose the trials, charting a clear road map to dynamically navigate the evolving world of social media. To ignore data is to leave these pieces unattended, only to wonder why the picture remains incomplete. The choice rests with you. Harness the power of data and step confidently towards your goal of creating viral social media content.

Chapter 10. Platform Peculiarities: Tailoring Content for Different Social Media Channels

Ever hung up on the enigma that, despite being armed with what appears to be a winning piece of content, it performs exceptionally well on one social media platform but utterly tanks on another? Fear not! Many a content creator has stumbled upon this contextual conundrum. The key is never about creating a piece of perfect content; rather, it's about carving content that's tailor-made for the specific platform it's allocated for. After all, each social media channel offers a unique blend of features, audience demographics, and usage styles that, when leveraged expertly, can turn into a goldmine for engagement.

10.1. Understanding Platform-Specific User Behavior

The basic groundwork to contextual content creation hinges on understanding the behavior of users on the individual platform. This refers to the manner in which they browse, engage, and react to content.

On Twitter, for instance, users are drawn to bite-sized chunks of information, owing to character limitations and the platform's rapid-fire content-sharing ethos. LinkedIn, conversely, is home to a largely professional demographic, seeking in-depth analyses, thought leadership content, and industry news. Instagram flourishes on visuals - stunning photographs and captivating videos that can narrate a story within an instant. Meanwhile, Facebook offers a wide-ranging demographic, making it suitable for various formats - from long-form articles to viral videos and everything in between. YouTube, as we all know, is the go-to hub for video content. It requires high-quality, original videos with potent storytelling capabilities.

By dissecting user behavior on various channels, content creators can shape their content to be more platform-appropriate, thereby enhancing its chances of virality.

10.2. Contouring Content According to Platform Mechanics

Every social media platform operates on a unique set of mechanics that favor particular types of content. Understanding these mechanics and constrictions is essential to content tailoring and improving its virality quotient.

Twitter's brisk-paced environment favors concise, impactful bursts of information, creating an ecosystem that thrives on shorter, snappy text or visual content coupled with trending hashtags. Instagram's picture-driven platform plays host to rich visual content focusing heavily on images, graphics, short videos or reels, and aesthetically pleasing grids. LinkedIn's professional networking milieu calls for industry insights, white papers, or thought-provoking articles, favoring a more formal tone and longer pieces of content. Facebook's dynamic ecosystem accommodates a broad variety of formats, making it a fertile zone for experimenting with diverse types of content. YouTube's user base is on the hunt for long-format videos that either entertain or educate.

Thus, aligning the form, tone, and pacing of the content according to the platform's inherent mechanics can significantly heighten engagement rates.

10.3. Leveraging Unique Platform Features for Content Customization

Every platform comes bundled with exclusive features that offer ample scope for creative customization. Twitter's threads and fleets, Instagram's stories and stickers, LinkedIn's polls, Facebook's mixed media formats or YouTube's end screens and annotations – these features, when used discerningly, can add nuance to your content while appealing to the platform's native user behavior.

10.4. Analytics for Platform-Specific Content Optimization

To sharpen your content strategy and create bespoke, platform-appropriate posts, it's essential to deepen your grasp over the data provided by each platform's analytics.

From Twitter's tweet activity and audience insights to Instagram's user engagement data, from LinkedIn's visitor analytics to Facebook's page insights, and from YouTube's watch time reports to viewer demographics, these rich data-sets provide an intimate peek into content performance. By examining the engagement metrics (likes, shares, comments, and more), the best performing content types, peak periods of user activity, and demographic information, content creators gain a very precise understanding of what works best on each platform.

In conclusion, the creation of viral social media content isn't a one-size-fits-all process. It requires a fine balance between understanding user behavior, platform mechanisms, unique features, and smart data-usage. By tailoring your content strategy to fit the demands and peculiarities of each platform, you inch closer to ruling the dynamic, ever-evolving world of social media.

Chapter 11. Case Studies of Viral Success: Learning from the Best in the Business

In the fascinating realm of social media, success is often a blend of strategic precision and sprinkling of creativity, riddled with elements of unpredictability. However, by examining a few noteworthy cases of successful viral campaigns, we can glean insights into practices that could potentially be emulated and integrated into our digital strategies. So, let's dive deep into these spectacular examples of triumph and tease out those valuable pearls of wisdom.

11.1. The ALS Ice Bucket Challenge: Harnessing the Power of Celebrity Influence and Novelty

An indelible instance of viral content success is the ALS Ice Bucket Challenge, which surfaced in the summer of 2014. The challenge was deceptively simple: individuals would film videos of themselves pouring ice-cold water over their heads and subsequently nominate friends to do the same. But the real victory was that each participation also encouraged donations to charities working towards ALS (Amyotrophic Lateral Sclerosis) research.

This particular campaign demonstrated two key elements of virality: novelty and the power of influential people. The concept was fresh, amusing, and comprised a challenge - a provocation for people to step out of their comfort zones. Add to this, the participation of celebrity figures who, with their large followings, sent the campaign trending rapidly across the globe. It's an envisioning that spotlights how unusual ideas coupled with impactful personalities can, as a union, spur significant digital engagement.

11.2. Dove's 'Real Beauty Sketches': Leveraging Emotion and Positive Messaging

Dove's 'Real Beauty Sketches' campaign set an admirable example in crafting heartfelt, positive messaging with the power to connect deeply with audiences. It portrayed women describing themselves to a forensic sketch artist who drew their portraits without actually seeing them. Later, acquaintances of these women would describe them to the same artist. The resulting sketches based on self-description were starkly different - and generally less flattering - compared to those based on others' descriptions, highlighting the skewed self-perception most women harbored about their beauty.

By addressing a social issue and leveraging emotional storytelling, Dove not only created content that resonated widely with its target audience but also bolstered its brand ethos as one that champions real beauty. The lesson here: content that taps into emotions, particularly when channeled towards a positive cause, has immense potential for virality.

11.3. Old Spice 'The Man Your Man Could Smell Like': The Magic of Humour and Creativity

Who can forget the Old Spice man, perched on his horse, promising to turn your average male into a suave, sophisticated gentleman? Launched during the Super Bowl, this ad was a delightful blend of humour, creativity, and unexpected twists that quickly morphed into a viral sensation. It demonstrated the appeal of comedic content, which not only entertains but also encourages sharing.

Through its innovative presentation, the ad successfully rebranded Old Spice, a traditional company, as hip and modern. The takeaway being that a good dose of creativity, spiced with humor, can deliver powerful results, etching a brand deeply into consumer memory.

11.4. Blendtec: Will it Blend?: The Art of the Unexpected

The 'Will it Blend?' series by Blendtec, although seemingly silly, was an ingenious strategy showcasing the power of their blenders in a fun, suspenseful format. Every week, founder Tom Dickson would attempt to blend various gadgets, from iPhones to glow sticks, thus demonstrating Blendtec's blending prowess.

This campaign exemplified the element of surprise as a driver of virality. The principle of 'unexpectedness' was intriguing enough to keep viewers coming back for more. The key takeaway: unpredictability can, indeed, be a valuable tool in your viral marketing toolkit.

In conclusion, while there is no prescribed formula for creating viral content, studying these examples provides valuable insights. Novelty, impactful personalities, emotional connectivity, humour, creative expression, positive messaging and unexpectedness are all influential drivers of engagement, capable of catapulting campaigns from mere whispers in the digital realm to powerful, globe-spanning conversations. As we comprehend these pivotal levers, we can begin to marshal our strategies, imbuing them with elements that have the potential to resonate meaningfully and powerfully with our audiences, thus charting our route towards viral success.